CW01645719

American Foreign Policy in Iraq

American Foreign Policy in Iraq

By: Dr. Saifaldin Z. AL-Darraji

Publisher: London Printing & Publishing

Printed by: MBG (INT) Ltd - London

LONDON
Printing • Publishing

First Edition 2021

ISBN: 978-1-912410-30-9

Printed & Published by:

London Printing & Publishing

Tel: 0044 (0) 20 7289 9009
info@londonbook.uk www.londonbook.uk
282 Harrow Road, London W2 5ES, UK

Sponsored by
Al-Mada Organization for Development
and Strategic Studies
www. al-mada.org
email: info@al-mada.org

American Foreign Policy in Iraq

From Obama to Trump: Troop Pull-Out and Counter-Terrorism

Dr. Saifaldin Z. AL-Darraji

Dedication

For my wife Inas and children, Mohammed and Ahmed

Acknowledgment

I owe special thanks to the department of politics, Birkbeck, University of London. In whose ideal environment the major part of the research and writing of this book was done.

To Prof. Alex Colas and Prof. Toby Dodge for their critical comments.

To Dr. Sevket Akyildiz and Dr. Gareth Jones, whose support and guidance were essential to its completion.

Dr. Saifaldin Z. AL-Darraji

London 2021

Table of Contents

Introduction

This book investigates the foreign policy of both the Obama and Trump administrations towards Iraq's national security and the influence both leaders had on that country. To do this, we will examine two core elements of the United States of America's (U.S.) foreign policy towards Iraq: troop pull-out and counter-terrorism. We will not consider oil and gas extraction, trade and business deals, or the legacy of war on the common Iraqi citizenry. The timeline for this research will start in 2008, the year in which Obama won the presidency and will end in 2020. The research is topical and valuable insight into whether the hegemonic protector of the 'free world', the United States, assisted or hindered the national security of Iraq. Indeed, we argue and will provide evidence in the following work, to show that the U.S. foreign policy both assisted and hindered national security in Iraq. This impacted on the post-war reconstruction of the economy and society. U.S. foreign policy was at times beneficial to the people of Iraq and at other times operating in the self-interest of Washington.

By investigating the liberal-democratic intentions of Obama and the (neo-)realist and the neo-isolationist stance of Trump, we can analyse the implementation of the U.S. foreign policy. It will also reveal how each leader interpreted the foreign policy. We also highlight the limits of U.S. power in Iraq, and the problematic nature of post-war Iraqi politics. In particular, the emergence of the Islamic State of Iraq and Syria (ISIS) uncovered the weakness of post-war Iraqi society and army. The study concludes by asserting that the U.S. foreign policy seems less interested in the Arab world except in a security context.

The primary research question is *What drives the United States' relationship with Iraq*? The secondary research questions we address are: *What are the national interests and ideology involved?*

How do Obama and Trump's views of national interest differ, and why? How does this influence troop pull-out and counter-terrorism in Iraq?

The research method chosen for this study is a critical review of the literature; this will involve analysis of the United States government online (primary) sources, and the academic (secondary) sources – books and articles – focused on our research questions. The study is qualitative and draws on existing research and documented works.

In Part One, we examine the theories and concepts that drive Washington's relationship with Iraq. We explore international relations (I.R.) theory on realism and liberalism and the national interest. We examine the role of liberal internationalism and realism and the U.S. government. Next, the meaning of 'national interest' is explored in terms of the United States and its ideology. Then the Obama drivers of policy and the Trump drivers of policy are reviewed.

In Part Two, 'Obama, U.S. Foreign policy, and Iraq' we discuss (i) the Obama administration, U.S. interests, and Iraq; (ii) Obama and Iraq and the *military pull-out* of 2011, and (iii) Obama and counter-terrorism in Iraq, and the emergence and defeat of ISIS. The USA completed the *withdrawal* of most of its military personnel that defeated Saddam Hussein from Iraq in December 2011. Approximately 120 soldiers remained in the country after 2011, attached to the U.S. Embassy in a small advisory role. Despite these problems, in November 2013 Obama met with the former Iraqi Prime Minister (PM) Nouri al Maliki to ensure that there would be a continuing partnership. Obama urged the Iraqi PM to be more inclusive of the Sunni minority population of Iraq. Obama discussed the possibility of Iraq passing an election law which would increase political participation for all. In 2014, there was a drastic change to Obama's foreign policy in Iraq following the rise of ISIS.

In Part Three, we explore (i) Trump's administration, U.S. foreign policy, national interest and Iraq; (ii) Trump and the removal of US Troops; and (iii) Trump and counter-terrorism in Iraq. (In the 2016 presidential campaign, Trump advocated that the United States should seize the oil from Iraq, to repay for the liberation of Iraq and its cost to U.S. taxpayer. This decision would require both an invasion and occupation.) Trump, on many occasions, has denounced Obama's foreign policy decisions—notably towards Iran. In January 2017, Trump issued an executive order banning the entry of all Iraqi citizens, as well as the citizens of six other Muslim-majority countries. Trump defended this policy, by saying he was defending the homeland from the threat of terrorism. At the same time, in 2017, he assisted with the defeat of ISIS in Iraq and Syria.

Sources consulted

This book uses the governmental archive of the United States of America (*state.gov*) for primary sources. Also, the online library of Obama (*Obama Whitehouse. archives*) provides us with documents about his foreign policy. Primary sources are available from: the Commission of America's National Interest, the Rand Corporation, and the Congressional Research Service.

In regards to the ideologies investigated in our paper, we read Tim Dunne, Milja Kurki, and Steve Smith's *International Relations Theories, Discipline and Diversity* (2016). They explain the nature of the world order and the political relations between nation-states. It informs the reader about national interest and states, and theoretical approaches on I.R. Michael Cox and Doug Stokes's *U.S. Foreign Policy* (2018) looks at I.R. theories about American foreign policy.

Colin Dueck's *The Obama Doctrine* (2015) debates Obama's foreign policy and the retrenchment of America's military overseas. The same work explains Obama's ambitious domestic objects. In contrast, Robert S. Singh's *After Obama: Renewing American Leadership, Restoring Global Order* (2016) says Obama's foreign policy was not as successful as it could have been. He explores how U.S. foreign policy has weakened the American made world system and relegated liberal values.

Richard Mansbach and James McCormick's *Foreign Policy Issues for America: The Trump Years* (2019) outlines Trump's foreign policy. It provides the book with an overview of U.S. interests and the challenges faced by Trump. Hal Brands' *American Grand Strategy in the Age of Trump* (2018) analyses U.S. foreign policy's present and future interests. This source is a good starting point to understand the dilemmas and uncertainties faced by Washington and Trump. Ben Connable 'Weighing U.S. Troop Withdrawal from Iraq: Strategic Risks and Recommendations' (2020) explains the potential strategic consequences affiliated with U.S. military withdrawal from Iraq. He suggests hypothetical policies that Washington might take; these policies refer to strategic objectives, national interests, and security in a Middle East and Iraqi context.

Donna Starr-Deelen's *Counter-Terrorism from the Obama Administration to President Trump* (2018) explores the Obama administration and its use of force in counter-terrorism, starting with a debate on the war criterion versus the police strategy. Furthermore, the work looks at how the Trump administration approaches national security policies within the context of counter-terrorism. Richard Conley's *Presidential Leadership and National Security* (2018) explores the long-term effects of executive decisions, diplomatic endeavours, and military actions of both Obama and Trump. Conley discusses the philosophical approach of the U.S. counter-terrorism strategy.

From Obama to Trump

Part 1: Theory and concepts that drive the U. S. relationship with Iraq

1.1 Ideologies

The following will define the concepts used in this study: 'liberalism' and 'realism' in the context of I.R. theory. The context relates to foreign policy (and grand strategy), and national interests. A secondary level analysis includes social constructivist theory. Also, this section defines 'national interest', and what this means in liberal international and realist theory on U.S. foreign policy.

'Liberalism' in politics advocates individual and human rights, democracy and popular sovereignty. It emerged from the political philosophy of the European Enlightenment, circa the 1700s, and the British Industrial Revolution of the 1800s. Liberalism sees human society as rational and progressive. Its economic paradigm is liberal-capitalism. The French (1789) and American (1776) revolutions have roots in radical liberalism (Brown et al., 2018, pp.325-25).

'Liberal internationalism' is a theory that emerged from liberalism. Its focus is the international behaviour of (liberal) states, and it includes foreign policy and national interest debates. The central idea is that liberal states seek to reform the international system by implementing liberal normative values, morality, and the establishment of global institutions. Its advocates say that interdependence, collective institutions, and democracy will create a more peaceful and rational global system. However, its critics accuse it of 'imperialism', coercion and paternalism.

In U.S. grand strategy (the vision of a state's national security goals), in the liberal international model, the aim is to keep that country in its preeminent position. It requires the United States to have a strong economy and industrial base, and a powerful military that can project force against America's adversaries while protecting its allies. Nonetheless, more recent adherents to 'muscular' liberal internationalism favour foreign interventions, putting constraints on U.S. adversaries by measures such as limited airstrikes and the use of special forces, and potentially state on state warfare. Some liberal internationalists, however, oppose significant military intervention. For example, Deudney and Ikenberry argue that many liberal internationalists living in Western countries condemned President G.W. Bush for his 'illegal' invasion of Iraq (2017). Other U.S. leaders have worked within the existing rules and norms and multilateral processes and institutions. Historically, the liberal hegemon approach has benefited the United States and the international order; indeed, that country has helped to build the world order (for example, the United Nations).

'Realism' in international politics is the opposite of idealism; it spans thinkers from Thucydides, Hobbes, Machiavelli, to Hans Morgenthau and Kenneth N. Waltz. Classical realists see a continuity between human nature and the political construction of the state. The 'neorealists' (new realists) see the international system as anarchic and argue it always has been thus. Consequently, states are created and act within this behavioural framework. The critical driver is power in politics and the state the key actor. It is a rational actor seeking to secure its national interests. The pursuit of power and the balance of power are processes that figure strongly in this approach. Neorealists highlight, especially after the fall of the Soviet Union in December 1991, the role of the United States as the unipolar power

(Brown, 2018, pp. 471-72).

'National interest' is a central tenet of realist theory that uses it, firstly, in defence of the nation-state in the anarchical international system ('national security interest' is a similar concept). Secondly, it is an analytical tool used to study foreign policy and external threats and constraints, treaties, other state power interests, geo-strategy, and trade.

In the 'grand strategy' of the realist school, the focus is to keep the United States unchallenged (economically, politically, and militarily) at the top of the global order (likewise with the liberal model). In the international system, peace is the result of U.S. power and leadership. Spreading democracy comes second to the national interest. Unilateralism by the United States, in this view, is acceptable if it advances U.S. interests.

'Off-shore balancing' is a concept linked with (neo-)isolationism, defined by Steven Walz and John Mearsheimer as a strategy to forego nation-building and maintain U.S. primacy going forward and protect freedoms at home. Some realists argue that the best approach for Washington is to preserve its power to deter future threats from China and Russia. Consequently, Washington should be more cautious when involving itself financially and militarily in foreign countries. They also say that other nation-states should be more proactive in managing and paying for their security (Cox and Stokes, 2012, pp.18-19).

'National interest': United States, and ideology

'National interest' means the intentions and ambitions of sovereign states, generally in foreign policy. The interests are political and economic, military, and cultural. The national interest determines government action based on planning and strategy. In I.R., it concerns state-to-state relations. States having similar or the same ideologies or institutions might hold similar or the same interests (Brown, 2018, p.324; Wu, 2017, pp.391-419). The foreign ministers, military strategists, economists, and academics analyse their nation's perceived interests and wants within a conceptual framework and decision-making process (Nuechterlein, 1976, pp.246-266). It is evident in the Trump' 'America First' language and noted in his National Security Strategy.[1]

It is worth going back to the late 1700s and 1800s, to understand the ideology of the U.S. national interest. In the wake of the 1776 Revolution that the American elite reached a philosophical consensus about domestic and international affairs. The elite's decision-making was influenced by political, economic, and cultural interests. Ideals also influenced them like sovereignty and nationhood, democracy, liberty, and equality. Also, shaping U.S. foreign policy is capitalism and free-market liberal economics and overseas markets. The U.S. elites advance their country's national in-

1. 'National Security Strategy of the United States of America' (2017) *The White House.gov*. Available at: https://www.whitehouse.gov/wp-content/uploads/2017/12/NSS-Final-12-18-2017-0905.pdf (Accessed 15 August 2020).

terest to protect values and ideals at home and overseas among allies (Hunt, 1998, pp. 125).

In the late 1990s, the U.S. foreign policy contained several national interests (listed below). The U.S.' Strategic Plan' (1997-2001) was written under President Clinton's tenure (1993 to 2001) and reflected his liberal internationalist stance. Nonetheless, it also reflects the dominant U.S. liberal capitalist ideology that has been present in U.S. foreign policy since 1776. The document highlights drivers of U.S. foreign policy:

> *'The world environment is filled with contradictions and competing needs. We are largely at peace yet we continue to face many crises. As economic, social, political, and technological forces transform our world, the challenges and opportunities facing the United States and our allies are numerous and complex.'*[1]

1. FY 1999-2000, 'Department of State Performance Plan National Interests', *U.S. Government* [online] Available at: https://1997-2001.state.gov/global/general_foreign_policy/00_perf_1.pdf [Accessed 10 June 2020].

According to the U.S. Department of State, the seven national interests which shape foreign policy goals are as follows –

- *National Security*
- *Economic Prosperity*
- *American Citizens and Border Security*
- *Law Enforcement,*
- *Democracy,*
- *Humanitarian Response*
- *Global Issues.*[1]

The Strategic Plan (1997 to 2001) reports: '*These national interests are interrelated and mutually reinforcing*'.[2] It also explains (building on earlier thinkers, like Kant) that 'peace' will promote economic prosperity in society. The plan says nations with free-markets have similar ideological values and promote cooperation. Modern liberal-democratic states are less likely to threaten the security interests of

1. Ibid, p.1.
2. Ibid, p. 1.

other nations, and they support free-trade and economic growth. It reads: '*Nations cooperating for their mutual security are more likely to deal effectively with our common interests in maintaining our global environment*.'[1]

This ideological approach, developed over the last 250 years, forms the basis of many western societies. Michael H. Hunt says that the United States ascendancy stems from an accumulation of economic strength, national interests, and its ability to seek international goals with deliberation and patience. Furthermore, the United States has experienced a degree of luck in terms of historical timing and its relatively 'isolated' geographical location (Hunt, 2013, p.308).

In terms of the U.S. grand strategy (its national security goals) there are some common trends notable in the early twentieth century. Leaders consider different grand strategies in response to international politics. However, it depends on whether a democratic or republi-

1. Ibid, p. 1.

can leader wins the national election and how they see international affairs. In general, the U.S. president has more say in foreign policy because his hands are restrained at home by the Senate and the House of Representatives (Congress). In this context, the grand strategy will need to, firstly, establish its intent and plan its finance. It will seek to deter offensive acts against the U.S. homeland and its allies. Sccondly, it will assess U.S. military responsibilities abroad, list priorities and goals and implementation procedures. Thirdly, it will outline burden-sharing with allies (MacDonald, 2018, p.34; Copeland, 1997, pp.105-112; Singh, 2019).

The U.S. politicians and society, at home and abroad, are aware that their society is historically unique and powerful in so many ways:

> '*Although America's international preeminence unavoidably evokes similarities to earlier imperial systems, the differences are more essential. They go*

> *beyond the question of territorial scope. American global power is exercised through a global system of distinctively American design that mirrors the domestic American experience*' (Brzezinski, 1997, p. 23).

Joseph S. Nye looks at the types of power projections that the United States can deploy as it creates its world order. Nye focuses on two different power types: soft and hard. In the analysis, hard power is economic or military pressure which coerces others to follow a specific way of action. By comparison, soft power, like cultural power, and it promotes the power of values and ideas. The latter works much more subtly; it tends to make others want what you have to offer. Soft power plays a role in upholding Washington's world order since others are influenced by the U.S. system and admire it (Mead, 2009).

Iraq (est. 1932) is one of the most important oil-producing and countries of the Middle East. Its capital city of Baghdad is an icon of Islamic civilization. Its strategic location close to Turkey, Israel, Iran, the Persian Gulf, and Saudi Arabia – in addition to its natural resources, and consumption of foreign goods and services – is significant enough for it to attract the interest of Washington. Consequently, U.S. politicians and business people advance their interests when they discuss or propose policy in Iraq. Iraqi-American government relations have witnessed successive periods of fluctuation caused by political and economic instability. However, a stable Iraq in the region, without conflict and socio-economic problems, will undoubtedly help to establish stability in the Middle East—and promote U.S. national interests.

Next, we discuss 'policy drivers', which are broad aims, targets or statements considered to be desirable by the various bodies of government.

1.2 Obama drivers of policy 2009 to 2017

In January 2009, Obama became the U.S. President. His first foreign policy announcement meant to repair the United States' image overseas, especially in the Arab Muslim societies (Palestine, Iraq, Syria, Egypt, Saudi Arabia). Obama sought to end the U.S. -led wars in Iraq and Afghanistan; establish better relations with Iran; develop new relations with Russia (especially over nuclear proliferation); and encourage China's cooperation on regional and global issues. Obama's liberal international perspective promoted open dialogue, stability and international institutions (Indyk, 2012, pp.23-43).

Some observers argue that Obama's main priority was not foreign policy, but domestic issues. Unlike most presidents since World War II, he dedicated less time to international politics, believing that international strategies are subordinate to domestic matters. Obama's foreign policy evolved in the context of how the American voters perceived it. The *Econo-*

mist observed in December 2012: '*Mr Obama and his team believe that his outstanding task is to secure a domestic legacy. Their fear is that foreign entanglements may threaten that goal.*'[1]

Leslie Gelb has argued '*there is no Obama doctrine at all*' (2012, p.20). However, Obama's foreign policy looked to decrease costs, reduce commitments, avoid new military interventions, and rethink the U.S. strategic footprint abroad. Obama believed that U.S. retrenchment (cutting costs and commitments) could assist domestic planning and resources—and would improve the U.S. economy. He advocated domestic reforms (healthcare) and 'nation-building at home'.[2]

Containment is another element of his strategy, for example, with North Korea, Iran, and

1. Ref no. 48: 'Lexington', *Economist*, December 1 (2012), cited in Dueck, C. (2017) *The Obama Doctrine: American Grand Strategy Today.* New York: Oxford University Press.
2. Obama, Barack. (2011) 'Remarks by the President on Afghanistan', June 22, cited in *Obama Whitehouse Archives.gov*. 2020. [online] Available at: https://obamawhitehouse.archives.gov/the-press-office/2011/06/22/remarks-president-way-forward-Afghanistan (Accessed 13 June 2020).

China. Furthermore, while regime change has been an element of Obama's administration, for instance, in Libya circa 2011, the U.S. intervention there came later than French and British intervention and was later regretted by Obama. Obama fostered integration through diplomatic contact and membership of international institutions; in addition to bargaining as a technique (Dueck, 2015, pp. 33-41).

The liberal internationalist outlook is present in Barack Obama's 2017 statement about U.S. foreign policy. It was evident in the outgoing President Obama's letter to incoming President Trump, dated 20th January 2017. Obama reminded Trump about the importance of friendly international relations for peace and prosperity –

> '*American leadership in this world really is indispensable… It's up to us, through action and example, to sustain the international order that's expanded steadily since the end of the Cold War, and upon which our own wealth and safety depend*' (Zameena, 2017).

1.3 Trump drivers of policy 2017 to present

Since the First World War, the American foreign policy of both the democratic and republican elites has generally been in support of 'liberal internationalism'. Since 1945, the liberal international order has experienced widespread support in American foreign policy. The Cold War against the Soviet Union intensified this reaching out to allies. This outward-looking stance nurtured and developed the existing global liberal-capitalist global system (Schweller, 2018, p.33). Globalisation exemplifies this dominant ideological model. However, in the wake of the 2008 world recession and a string of problematic wars in Afghanistan and Iraq, Trump and his right-of-centre populist followers questioned the logic of the liberal establishment. Some of his white working-class and middle-class voters felt left behind by globalisation. They worry about employment opportunities, the wholesale redeployment of industries to China, the ethnic change in the U.S cities with the arrival of Mexican, Asian, African, and Muslim migrants.

Trump responds negatively to liberal America. He criticises the pillars of liberal internationalism and the policies of Obama. Seeing the world from a realist and (neo-)isolationist stance, and because of his bombastic personal style, he drops trade agreements with allies and advances a U.S. protectionist agenda. Trump sees other countries taking advantage of the United States. In his transactional mindset, it is imperative when dealing with other nations for the United States to be the winner. Unlike the liberal internationalists, he is suspicious of free trade. He complains in public about the growing economic power and human rights abuses of the Chinese Communist Party.

Trump mobilises his voters by deploying populism; his rhetoric emphasises: '*America first*'. Several social and cultural challenges have become pressing in the United States, such as racism, gender politics, and identity politics. Indeed, these topics and the economy seem to have polarised the American electorate. Nevertheless, Trump successfully used social and economic issues to win an election in 2016. At the same time, he blamed external actors like China and terrorists for America's domestic problems.

Substate groups (like multinational companies, and lobby groups) actively seek to affect state policy and power. Oil and gas companies, private security providers, and the pro-Zionist evangelical Christian Church, and others, seek to influence the U.S. foreign policy for their ends.

In his grand strategy, Trump disputes the relevance of NATO, particularly the U.S. financial contributions. Also, he questions the logic of 'America's alliance commitments' and foreign interventions, like the Iraq War (2003) (MacDonald, 2018a, pp.401-434). He sees the United Kingdom, Israel and Saudi Arabia as key trading partners. The sale of U.S. made weapons to Saudi Arabia is actively sought by Trump for U.S. financial gain, and to create jobs in the U.S. and to counterbalance China's military sales. He ended Obama's agreement with Iran about nuclear technology, which some observers say might increase the risk of drawing the United States into war. However, Donald Trump fired John Bolton, who was in favour of war with Iran and more U.S. military involvement in Iraq.

Notwithstanding, he is willing to increase spending on defence to combat terrorism and rogue states—and prevent the spread of nuclear weapons. He has used missiles and airstrikes to attack Syria's pro-Assad forces over their use of chemical weapons on civilians. Indeed, Trump sees the United States as an unbiased peacemaker.

Magcamit uses a three-way model that links populism, securitisation, and realist foreign policy to explain Trump's worldview. His 'populist securitisation' and leadership-style is a combined plan to justify his realist foreign policy. However, he might trigger 'illiberal tendencies' among some of his supporters at home (2017, pp.6-35).

The international community has been urged by Trump to share the burden in tackling risks and threats around the world. He says the allies of the United States should be partners in the confrontation against the threats faced by his administration, specifically militant Islamism, Iran and nuclear technology, and North Korea's nuclear bombs (Brands, 2018, p.169). Indeed, the strategic situation is fluid, and the United States faces an increasingly complex and unpredictable world in which the threats might become interconnected (ecological problems and climate change, terrorism, and civil wars). With regards to the above, the U.S. national policy and planning need to assess the capabilities, activities, and intentions of states and non-state actors in order to identify both risks and opportunities for U.S. national interests.

In the context of the Middle East and Iraq, the question for Trump is in balancing geostrategic security and interests. However, he is also looking further East.

> ‘*The 2018 National Defense Strategy (NDS) adds a new element, as it asserts that the United States will shift its military focus from countering terrorism toward great-power competition with, primarily, China and Russia*’ (Connable, 2020, p. 2).

Part 2: Obama, U.S. foreign policy, and Iraq

⊙ In Part Two, we discuss, firstly, Obama's administration, U.S. foreign policy and Iraq. We will assess the liberal influences in his policy. Secondly, the study will explore the decision by Obama in 2011 to pull U.S. troops out of Iraq. At this moment, ISIS emerged from the civil war in Syria and commenced seizing territories in Iraq. Thirdly, we consider the capture of Iraq's second city, Mosul by ISIS on the 10 June 2014, and consequently, Obama's counter-terrorism strategy in Iraq, and his role in defeating ISIS.

2.1 Obama, foreign policy, U.S. interests, and Iraq

In comparison with President Bush, the change in U.S. foreign policy under President Obama since 2009 has been a matter of contention. After two terms of U.S. foreign policy under Bush, involving the projection forcc overseas unilaterally and in defence of U.S. national interests, Obama's approach to foreign and security policy appeared non-interventionist. His administration focused on internal affairs (Lindsay, 2011, p.772). Importantly, Obama believed that Washington could not solve problems in the Middle East and that Middle Easterners should manage with their affairs. This position is remarkably similar to that of Trump, which we discuss later. There is a small difference worth mentioning here, both men preferred limited counter-terrorism efforts, and 'off-shore balancing' over nation-building; however, Trump seeks to change the spending commitments of allies, rather than 'sharing'. Obama was sceptical that the United States could influence the Middle East, and his remarks to the UN General Assembly (September 2013) make this clear. That year, terrorist violence in Iraq increased, and sectarian tension worsened–Obama says:

'Efforts to resolve sectarian tensions that continue to surface in places like Iraq, Bahrain and Syria. We understand such longstanding issues cannot be solved by outsiders; they must be addressed by Muslim communities.'[1]

After the painful experience of two costly wars in Iraq (and Afghanistan), with U.S. taxpayers, military personnel, and Iraqi and Afghan citizens taking the main burden, Obama believed that military operations had to be lim-

1. 'President Obama in Address to the United Nations General Assembly', *White House Website*. 23 September, 2013. Available at: https://obamawhitehouse.archives.gov/the-press-office/2013/09/24/remarks-president-obama-address-united-nations-general-assembly (Accessed 15 August 2020).

ited. He concentrated on the defence of vital U.S. interests and multilateral security options (Fawaz, 2013, p.301). In brief, under Obama, it was not the aim of U.S. foreign policy that altered, rather the means chose to deliver them (Manyin, 2018, p.4).

In his speech of the State of Union, 2010, Obama supports the belief that American liberal values should relate to foreign policy actions:

> 'As we have for over 60 years, America takes these actions because our destiny is connected to those beyond our shores. But we also do it because it is right. (...) For America must always stand on the side of freedom and human dignity--always. (...) Abroad, America's greatest source of strength has always been our ideals'.[1]

1. Obama, Barack (2010) 'Address before a Joint Session of the Congress on the State of the Union', January 27. *Obama Whitehouse Archives.gov.* [online] Available at: https://obamawhitehouse.archives.gov/the-press-office/remarks-president-state-union-address (Accessed 16 June 2020).

The world financial crisis, circa 2008, affected Obama's foreign policy, and the United States' international economic position. The consequence of the financial crisis went far beyond money issues; the United States had far more of a difficulty in holding itself up to the world as a dominant (capitalist) economic model. Obama's liberal view of the world problem-solving and America's role in it were shaped by his generational understanding and by the events shaped his political career. Importantly, Obama came out strongly against Bush's war in Iraq (Mann, 2012, p.73).

2.2 Obama and Iraq: military pull-out 2011

Obama found himself stuck in two inherited costly wars in Iraq and Afghanistan and handed an economy in crisis. Also, criticism of U.S. foreign policy in the Middle East and Latin America rose both at home and abroad at the time he took office. Obama needed to make a gesture to show his administration was going to be different to Bush's.

The Bush administration in 2008 negotiated a Status of Forces Agreement (SOFA) with the government of Iraq, to withdraw all U.S. forces from Iraq at the end of 2011 but potentially, to keep some forces behind for training of Iraq soldiers. An early critic of Bush's decision to invade Iraq in 2003, Obama pledged during the 2008 election campaign to withdraw the troops as soon as possible. In February 2009, he planned to bring U.S. troop levels down in Iraq from 160,000 to 50,000 by August 2010—including the departure of all combat forces. The rest of the troops, he continued, would be withdrawn by the end of 2011. For many years, the withdrawal progressed smoothly, in part because Obama was able to build on the gains accomplished by Bush's 'surge' of 20,000 additional troops in 2007, which had supported the government of Iraq to restore some degree of stability in the country. By 2012, Approximately 120 American troops were in Iraq, a number that stayed for about three years; this was part of the Office for Security Cooperation-Iraq, which effectively facilitated weapons transfers to the Iraqi government (Lindsay, 2011, p. 772).

Obama's critics argue that although the situation was unstable in Iraq, as the deadline drew nearer, the administration should have made more efforts to renegotiate the SOFA and hold American troops in place (Brennan, 2014). They claim that the failure to do so resulted from the president's preference for leaving Iraq, rather than an effort to find a compromise and they blame the withdrawal as a major cause for the rise of ISIS. Officials in the Obama administration requested Iraqi PM Maliki and his government to rethink the SOFA to allow for a force of up to 10,000 to remain to support Iraqi sovereignty. The PM Maliki cabinet and the Iraqi parliament struggled to decide on this informal offer before late 2011, leaving U.S. troops to withdraw under the 2008 SOFA (Kahl, 2014). However, Iraqi security forces were not ready to control Iraq's security needs. The quality of the soldiers and the weaknesses in the command and control of the Iraqi security forces raised uncertainties about the military's ability to operate professionally after a drawdown of the U.S. troops from Iraq (Dodge, 2012).

As a consequence, withdrawing most U.S. troops from Iraq weakened America's ability to respond to events in the region. Later, Obama proved that his policy towards Iraq was not so rigid. He redeployed hundreds of U.S. military soldiers to support the Iraqi military forces battle against ISIS (Glaser, 2017, p.8).

Before the fight against ISIS, the Iraqi state was not functioning effectively. It had experienced interethnic and inter-communal tensions, a weak economy, and a demoralised police and army. (We discuss this further below.) Vali Nasr worked at the State Department at the time and wrote the book *The Dispensable Nation* (2014).[1] He says that Iraq's:

1. *Congressional Record,* United States of America Senate.

> '… fragile power-sharing arrangement… required close American management. But the Obama administration had no time or energy for that. Instead, it anxiously eyed the exits, with its one thought to get out. It stopped protecting the political process just when talk of American withdrawal turned the heat back up under the long-simmering power struggle that pitted the Shias, Sunnis, and Kurds against one another'.[1]

Josh Rogin says the Obama administration had decided to withdraw U.S. forces from Iraq, and he sought to calm the opposition Republican Party. They were in favour of keeping a small U.S. military presence, by pretending to continue negotiations with the Iraqi

(2014) Vol. 160, Part 8, June 23, p.11127. [online] Available at: https://books.google.co.uk/books?id=1V5cpDql_eUC&printsec=frontcover&source=gbs_ge_summary_r&cad=0#v=onepage&q&f=false (Accessed 16 June 2020), p. 11127. See also 'National Security Strategies of the United States of America', *Obama Whitehouse Archives.gov.* (2015), p.180. [online] Available at: https://obamawhitehouse.archives.gov/sites/default/files/docs/2015_national_security_strategy_2.pdf (Accessed 16 June 2020).

1. Ibid.

government. Rogin reports the views of Iraqi and American officials who explain how the decision to push a SOFA through parliament – which contained immunity for U.S. forces – was Washington's decision. Also, officials from both sides believed this request would ruin any chance of continued U.S. military presence.[1]

The following section on counter-terrorism policy in Iraq, and the emergence of ISIS in that country, as we shall see, and some analysts argue, is directly linked to the flawed and ill-considered troop pull-out strategy. Obama's desire to bring the troops home, while admirable, provided ISIS with a free hand in Iraq.

2.3 Obama and counter-terrorism, and defeating ISIS

Before we discuss Obama's counter-terror-

1. Rogin, Josh (2011), *Foreign Polcy.com.* Available at: https://foreignpolicy.com/2011/10/21/how-the-obama-administration-bungled-the-iraq-withdrawal-negotiations/ (Accessed 15 August 2020).

ism strategy against ISIS, we will briefly define the concept of 'terrorism'. This is followed by describing how the new Iraq appeared to outsiders and the Iraqis several years after liberation. In brief, some analysts saw Iraq at this time as a 'failing state'. These two topics give meaning to the broader debate emergence and aims of ISIS.

Before the analysis of Obama's counter-terrorism strategy in Iraq, we will define our terms and concepts on the topic. There is no agreed academic definition of 'terrorism'; however, our book uses Jones and Libicki's working political definition of a terrorist group: '*a collection of individuals belonging to a non-state entity that uses terrorism to achieve its objectives*' (2007, p.3). We use this in connection with Ayse Zarakol's definition of terrorism. She helps us understand the concept of the 'non-state' terror group(s) by explaining that the modern state '*displaced three types of authority with competing legitimacy claims: religious, localized and personal*'

(2011, pp.2311-2336). Zarakol argues that the terrorist groups claim legitimacy based on a past injustice involving their displacement by the modernising state. This is especially useful for explaining the rise of ISIS. ISIS, unlike other extremist political groups, do not seek to build a modern 'state', but instead, a global 'caliphate'. In this regard, Obama's scepticism of their being a military solution to ISIS seems justified. He sees the need for political and education to change the hearts and minds of the extremists (as we discuss further below).

In order to understand the speed of the ISIS advance in Iraq, it is worth explaining the poor condition of the Iraqi government and society at the time. In 2013, in Iraq, ISIS was initially successful with territorial gains, gathering resources, and using modern communication technologies and social media. However, in Iraq, it found a weakened society that was fragmented and unable to counterattack. In the post-war and 'nation-state building' environment of Iraq, circa 2003, there was Sunni and Shi'a sectarian mistrust and tension. But arguably just as crucial for local cooperation, there was the internal division within Shia and Sunni groups, the latter being particularly important for the spread of ISIS taking over Sunni provinces, as tribes competed for political influence.[1] The Iraqi security services were war-weary. The Iraqi Kurds were not sufficiently trained and prepared to take on battle-hardened ISIS guerrilla fighters arriving from successes against Assad's forces in Syria.

U.S. returns

The capture of Iraq's second city, Mosul by ISIS on the 10th June 2014 was ISIS's largest offensive to date. Its militants killed hundreds of Shi'a inmates from the Badoush prison during the attack. On the 18th June 2014, Iraq asked the United States to use airstrikes

1. Tollast, Robert. 'The civil wars of Iraq's Sunni tribes.' 2016. *1001 Iraqi Thoughts*.com, 28 March. Available at: https://1001iraqithoughts.com/2016/03/28/the-civil-wars-of-iraqs-sunni-tribes-fault-lines-within-8-sunni-tribes-and-sub-tribes-2003-2016/ (Accessed 15 August 2020).

against ISIS, following a massacre of 1,700 Shia air force cadets at the former U.S. army base, Camp Speicher. This led Obama to issue some very reserved statements, attempting to reassure the U.S. public that the U.S. military was not going to war in Iraq all over again. He had already remarked on 13 June 2014: '*It's fair to say that, in our consultations with the Iraqis, there will be some short-term, immediate things that need to be done militarily*' (Mason, 2014). In the same month of June 2014, Obama attempted to reassure the U.S. public, explaining that ISIS was primarily an Iraqi problem:

> '... this is not solely or even primarily a military challenge. Over the past decade, American troops have made extraordinary sacrifices to give Iraqis an opportunity to claim their own future. Unfortunately, Iraq's leaders have been unable to overcome too often the mistrust and sectarian differences that have long been simmering there, and that's created vul-

> nerabilities within the Iraqi government as well as their security forces.'[1]

It is clear that the rise of ISIS challenged Obama's security strategy transition in Iraq, risking a new U.S. military commitment and the use of hard power for what he believed was a political and ideological problem. Arguably, any need to bomb ISIS might have been avoided had greater security cooperation been in place before 2014. The fact that Iraq was not able to defeat the ISIS terrorists alone suggests that American troops left too soon.

From controlling a small part of Iraq's territory in 2013, ISIS and its extremist supporters became the major threat to American interests in the timespan one year. ISIS violence threatened the Arab and non-Arab political order in the Middle East. However, it is important to consider in the case of Iraq that Obama ap-

1. (2014) 'White House Office of the Press Secretary. Statement by the U.S. President on Iraq', *Obama Whitehouse. Archives. gov.* 13 June. Available at: https://obamawhitehouse.archives.gov/the-press-office/2014/06/13/statement-president-iraq (accessed 15 August 2020).

peared to believe the United States did not need to have troops in Iraq for counter-terror actions.

Initially, the Iraqis received limited help, largely due to Obama's dislike of Maliki and a feeling that Iraq was not a foreign policy issue he wanted to revisit. The fight against ISIS changed the narrative of Obama's foreign policy, but importantly, the fight did not change the philosophy of Obama's foreign policy. He still did not want to enter foreign wars.

Obama's initial delay in action enabled ISIS to gain ground. An explanation for this is that Obama feared deeper 'counter-terrorism' operations would turn his limited involvement in Iraq into a bigger war. For example, in August 2014, when U.S. airstrikes were used in Iraq, to protect Yazidis from 'ethnic cleansing' or worse, and to protect Shi'a, and to protect the Mosul Dam, the aim was not a campaign to defeat ISIS. Obama explained: '*There's no American military solution to the larger crisis in Iraq. The only lasting solution is reconcili-*

ation among Iraqi communities and stronger Iraqi security forces.'[1] This delay in a larger airstrike campaign led ISIS to build up its money, capability, strength and weapons in Syria and facilitated its transit into Iraq (Singh, 2016, p.32).

Obama advanced the international liberal model further by cooperating with the new Iraqi democratic leader. Obama slowly increased counter-terrorism cooperation in Iraq. In April 2015, PM Haidar al Abadi visited the White House and, with Obama, released a joint statement on the U.S.-Iraq Strategic Partnership based respect and common interests. Both parties said they would deal with terror threat and extremism.[2] Indeed, U.S. airstrikes increased against ISIS, and more U.S. troops

1. (2014) 'President Obama Makes a Statement on the Crisis in Iraq', *Obama White House Archives.gov.* 14 August. Available at: https://obamawhitehouse.archives.gov/blog/2014/08/07/president-obama-makes-statement-iraq (Accessed 15 August 2020).
2. (2015) 'Joint Statement by the United States of America and the Republic of Iraq', *Obama White House Archives.gov.* April 14. https://obamawhitehouse.archives.gov/the-press-office/2015/04/14/joint-statement-united-states-america-and-republic-iraq (Accessed 15 August 2020).

sent to the country.

In Iraq, the American built and led multinational coalition was ultimately successful in stopping the ISIS advances. Leading a coalition of over allied 60 countries, with the backing of the Gulf Cooperation Council (GCC), Obama assured that the U.S.-led coalition operations were not another ground war in the Middle East. In consideration of the situation and the removal of U.S. troops from Iraq, Obama turned a foreign policy oversight into a military success (Santos and Teixeira, 2015, p119-145).

Obama's 'Address Before a Joint Session of the Congress on the State of the Union', 20 January 2015, reported:

> 'American leadership-including our military power-is stopping ISIL's advance. Instead of getting dragged into another ground war in the Middle East, we are leading a broad coalition, including Arab nations, to degrade and ultimately de-

stroy this terrorist group.'[1]

In the same year, Obama said:

> 'The United States and GCC member states further affirmed their commitment to assisting the Iraqi government and the international coalition in their fight against ISIL/DAESH.' [2]

Obama's approach to extremism

When he came to office, President Obama was determined to settle a seemingly unending war on terrorism. He vowed to make his counter-terrorism policies more 'transparent and ethical' than Bush's administration, but

1. ________(2015) 'Remarks By The President In State Of The Union Address', *Whitehouse.gov*, January 20, [online] Available at: https://obamawhitehouse.archives.gov/the-press-office/2015/01/20/remarks-president-state-union-address-January-20-2015 [Accessed 4 July 2020].
2. Obama, Barack. (2015) 'U.S.--Gulf Cooperation Council Camp David Joint Statement', 14 May 2015, cited in *Obama Whitehouse Archives.gov. The White House United States*. [online] Available at: https://obamawhitehouse.archives.gov/realitycheck/the-press-office/2015/05/14/us-gulf-cooperation-council-camp-david-joint-statement [Accessed 15 June 2020].

this also contrasts starkly with Trump who advocated torture of terrorists – Obama firmly opposed it – and targeting their families. In an attempt not to use the excessive force that had characterised Bush's regime, Obama relied on an accumulation of targeted killing by drones, and the U.S. security services and special forces in support of allies (like the Iraqi and Kurdish forces).

Also, Obama increased the selective use of targeted electronic surveillance. In the knowledge management sphere, Obama differed from Trump in that he explored the underlying social and political reasons for terrorism. This willingness to look at the complexity of terrorism probably stems from his socially liberal outlook and his academic background.

Obama took office under challenging conditions: the United States had been at war for seven years (in Afghanistan and Iraq, and was battling global terrorism). In the Iraqi reconstruction project that Bush and Obama tried to facilitate, their efforts were thwarted by civil war and sectarian conflicts. During Obama's two terms in office (eight years in duration) he was a 'war president' fighting terrorism, using military force in Libya, Yemen and Somalia. Yet, in each of these cases, it could be argued that interventions were influenced by an off-shore balancing mindset, quite different to the military occupations favoured by Bush and in this regard, not dissimilar to the smaller interventions favoured by Trump.

In handling the terrorist threat, some argue that Obama's approach, unlike Bush and his neoconservative advisors, has sometimes erred too far towards idealism? Notwithstanding Obama's laudable efforts to carefully calibrate Washington's response to meet a seemingly small, but problematic terrorist threat did not create a more secure world. The American people found themselves living in a world with more terrorism, not less. Radical Islamism expanded during and after the U.S. led wars in Afghanistan and Iraq. The rise of ISIS suggests the failure of Bush's policies of counter-terrorism; and it informed Obama's decision to withdraw the U.S. troops from Iraq. Bush's emotional language of 'global war on terrorism' was replaced by Obama's more considered 'countering violent extremism' approach (Jenkins, 2017, pp.1-5).

In consideration of ISIS, it is fair to ask whether Obama's updated strategy, which involved heavier use of airstrikes and special forces (in contrast to his weaker early intervention in 2014) was any better than Bush's model? Obama's strategy was one of containment; training and equipping of the anti-ISIS adversaries in Iraq and Syria and stopping the flow of pro-ISIS foreign fighters into ISIS territory.

In attempting to erode and eliminate the allure of extremist ideologies, Obama has tried to magnify anti-extremist voices who can produce an Islamic counter-argument to the jihadist-Islamist agenda. Here Islamic intellectuals and Muslim clerics from all over the world and ex-jihadists play a vital role, who reject the idea that terrorist groups such as ISIS act 'Islamic'. Moderate and liberal clerics and those who were once involved with extremism, and since reformed, are can inform a western audience about the jihadist mentality. Obama's approach to counter-terrorism explores preventative policies which might prove to be the best way to combat and reduce jihadism in the long-term. So, we can say that Obama's liberal-influenced approach tried to find a longer-term and cooperative solution to extremist groups who feel threatened by modernity and globalisation.

This is because it is unlikely that radical Islamism will be defeated by either hard or soft power alone. The jihadist threat needs a steadily evolving response that uses both hard and soft power (Stern, 2015, pp.62-70). The United States remains 'the' superpower (Marshall, 2019, p.76), and its counter-terrorism policy has undergone significant changes since 11 September 2001. Actions such as pre-emptive war, the use of 'enhanced' interrogation techniques, the indefinite detention of terrorism suspects, and the use of targeted killings by armed drones have been used in Bush's 'war on terrorism'. Some argue that, the United States makes the world a safer place (Pilecki, 2014, pp.285-299).

With this in mind, the continuing problems of the U.S. national security in Iraq, the issue of troop withdrawal and extremist Islamists were a challenge for Obama throughout the last two years of his presidency. They also cast a long shadow on Trump's administration from 2017 onwards (Starr-Deelen, 2018). Indeed, it could be argued that since 2011, both Obama and Trump have been involved in debates on how light footprint the U.S. military involvement in Iraq should be. However, their preference is to pull back substantially from the Middle East.

Terrorism: legacy

The following section will consider how

terrorism has become linked with Muslims by political elites. The constructivist theory emphases perceptions and ideas and how they might shape policy.

McCrisken argues that Bush's 'war on terror' has become institutionalised within the American psyche. In turn, a set of assumptions are made about Muslims, Islam, and the Middle Eastern peoples. Americans, in general, do not consider sectarian differences, like Shi'a and Sunni. As a result, negative stereotypes drive foreign policy-making (2011, pp. 781-801). It is difficult to deny that the 'war on terror' has shaped a generation of Americans. The 'war on terror' in principle is a constructed idea (Kayser, 2015, pp.50-53). Attitudes about the 'war on terror' do not adjust with either realist or liberal theories. In contrast, social constructivism provides us with a way to understand how structures are social rather than material, and those structures form interests, not just behaviour (Wendt, 1995, pp. 71-81).

Today, the terrorist enemies of the United

States, like radical Islamist organisations, function globally, violate borders, and radicalise citizens and through the internet. Terrorists use violence or the threat of it to put pressure on the U.S. interests and challenge U.S. power.[1] Yet, the United States remains the world's most capable military power, with a unique capacity to project power on a global basis (International Institute Strategic Studies, 2020, p.45). It includes counter-terrorism strategies and implementation. In his address to Congress after the terror attacks of 11 September 2001, Bush declared that: '... *our war on terror begins with al-Qaida, but it does not end there. It will not end until every terrorist group of global reach has been found, stopped, and defeated*'.[2]

1. *National Strategy for Counterterrorism of The United States of America*, (2018) U.S. Whitehouse, Washington, pp.1-35. [online] Available at: https://www.google.com/search?q=national+strategy+for+counterterrorism+of+the+united+states+of+america+october+2018&rlz=1C1GGRV_enGB750GB750&oq=National+Strategy+for+Counterterrorism+of+the+United+States+of+America+october&aqs=chrome.0.0j69i57.9945j0j7&sourceid=chrome&ie=UTF-8 [Accessed 19 June 2020].
2. U.S. Department of State, 2009-2017, *Patterns of Global Terrorism*. President Bush address to Congress on September 20,

Eight years later, Obama addressed the nation after the failed Christmas 'underwear bomber' event (of 25 December 2009): '*We are at war. We are at war against al-Qaeda, a far-reaching network of violence and hatred that attacked us on 9/11, that killed nearly 3,000 innocent people, and that is plotting to strike us again*' (King, 2016, p. 136).

Obama disagreed with core elements of the Bush administration's 'war on terror' relating to the prison at Guantanamo Bay (Cuba), interrogation and water-boarding, intrusive surveillance, and the killing of suspected terrorists. Obama's inaugural address says '*we reject as false the choice between our safety and our ideals*'; furthermore, it reflects his liberal world outlook and, as shown below, stands in stark contrast with the views of Donald Trump. It highlights their different views of Iraqi society and its people (Dueck, 2015, p.44).

2001, Washington. [online] Available at: https://2009-2017.state.gov/j/ct/rls/pgtrpt/index.htm [Accessed 19 June 2020].

Al-Qaeda remains active despite having been reduced in size, strength and influence by the United States and its allies. The rise of ISIS in 2014 in Iraq and Syria and the establishment of the so-called Islamic State territory presented a new security risk to the international order. ISIS, for a few years, eclipsed the threat from al-Qaeda.

Part 3: Trump administration, U.S. Interests, and Iraq

In Part Three, we explore: (i) Trump's administration, U.S. foreign policy, national interest, and Iraq; (ii) Trump and the removal of US Troops from Iraq; and (iii) Trump and counter-terrorism in Iraq.

3.1 Trump, U.S. foreign policy, national interest and Iraq

The strategic interests of Washington in Iraq have not always been apparent; they have been notoriously complex. Factors that make analysis difficult include the nature of the 2003 Iraq War, the post-war reconstruction in Iraq, competition from the regional powers, and the emergence of ISIS. A Rand Corporation document (2020) says:

> 'One of the most oft-stated concerns about the continuing U.S. military presence in Iraq is the perceived lack of a clear regional or country-specific strategy to guide military purpose and action. We agree that strategic clarity on Iraq is much needed, and we find that the stated official objectives are not sufficiently linked to consistent policies or justifications for U.S. military operations. Since the 2003 U.S.-led coalition invasion of Iraq, some Iraq policies appear to have been directly at odds with contemporaneous strategic statements' (Connable, 2020, p. 3).

While policy and strategy lack coordination, the main aim of U.S. national interests between 2003 and 2020 has been to make Iraq an independent and democratic country, liberal-capitalist in its economy, and make it a sustainable polity. But there is little agreement on the role of the U.S. or Iraqi military in this.

By 2011, in consideration of ongoing Iraqi development policies, and with the backing of the independent Iraqi government, and in response to the U.S. voters' call to 'bring our troops home', the U.S. military presence in Iraq was scaled back.

This is despite the realisation by the United States and Iraq that a military pull-out was not necessarily in the best security interests for all parties and that Iraq was not fully prepared to manage its security commitments on its borders and internally. Nonetheless, regional powers worked to influence events in Iraq, in particular Iran, an important consideration for the United States. In 2017, Iraq experienced similar social unrest and weak government as it did in 2011. The question remained, were the United States and coalition forces still needed?

The Trump administration, despite its realist and neo-isolationist tendencies, had to balance its interests in Iraq (including access to oil contracts and the selling of U.S. goods and services) with regional security and relations with regional powers (like Turkey, Iran, Israel, and Saudi Arabia). Like Obama, the new leader Trump realised Iraq could not be quickly abandoned.

In 2019, the U.S. Department of State repeated its objectives in Iraq (first declared under Bush) –

> 'Iraq is now a key partner for the United States in the region as well as a voice of moderation and democracy in the Middle East… U.S. security assistance supports the development of a modern, accountable, fiscally sustainable, and professional Iraqi military capable of defending Iraq and its borders' (Connable, 2020, p. 4).

In early 2020, and consideration of the

above, one Rand publication explained that:

> 'Given the variability between stated strategic objectives and the practical policies on Iraq, and given the shifting global environment, we distilled a set of five U.S. national security interests from recent and current policy documents to help drive our analysis' (Connable, 2020, p.3).

The five security interests were firstly, to defeat ISIS both militarily and economically. Furthermore, to use counter-terrorism against it, and to work with allies to defeat it. Secondly, to counter Iran in Iraq and the wider region (Yemen), and to prevent Iran from sponsoring terrorism. Also, to stop Iran from developing nuclear technology and weapons. Thirdly, to compete with China and Russia in terms of political, economic and military influence in the region. The United States sees both countries as threats to its interests in the Middle East. Fourthly, the United States supports the economic development of Iraq to improve the lives of the masses. Also, to prevent the exploitation of the young Iraqis by the militant jihadists; the latter mobilise alienated Iraqis based on longstanding economic injustices and sectarian narratives. Fifthly, the United States wishes to ensure its regional military presence and dominance. So, by having the U.S. military deployed in the region, Trump is acting to secure regional stability and maintain order (Allison, 2020).| (The United States has an airbase in Turkey and close relations with Israel and Saudi Arabia.)

Nonetheless, Trump wished to remain engaged in Iraq in the most cost-efficient way, and this, rather than any guiding ideological approach, has driven considerations. As Anthony Cordesman explains, the United States spends $700 billion a year on the military, but under Trump, there seems to be no real strategy in any geographical region. The focus has turned from counter-terrorism to containment of Iran, and potential conflicts with China (and Russia). Other priorities include arms sales and burden-sharing. Cordesman says:

> 'The U.S. has minimized the importance of strategic partnerships, undermined or rejected serious arms control efforts, and focused on strategic partner and allied total military spending to the near exclusion of an interest in maintaining and strengthening key strategic partnerships' (Cordesman, 2020).

Cordesman reports that Iraqi trust in Washington has diminished because the removal of U.S. forces in Iraq, only for them to return later. On the other hand, Trump has been impatient with Iraq, as evidenced by his early statements during the war on ISIS, which he said overwhelming military power would resolve.

3.2 Trump and military pull-out

Since 2003, the United States has provided around $20bn for Iraq's armed forces. Washington intended to make Iraq a reliable ally in the regional security balance. However, all of that came under threat on the 3 January 2020 when a U.S. drone killed Iran Quds Force commander-in-chief, Qasem Soleimani, in Baghdad. The Iraqi government, in shock, wished to express their displeasure with the Trump government and called for all U.S. forces to be removed from Iraq. Consequently, the United States and Iraq entered into a new 'Strategic Dialogue' about their security relationship and U.S. troops on the ground (Hannah and Zarif, 2020). In terms of national interest, both parties need to reflect upon the situation and consider the other's stance (Dixit and Nalebuff, 1993, pp.33-34). Trump has said that it is not the right time for the U.S. troops to withdraw from Iraq (Sink and Carey, 2020). Furthermore, in his recent 2020 address, Secretary Pompeo reported:

> 'As a force for good in the nation and as Iraq's closest friend, the United States has proposed a Strategic Dialogue with the Government of Iraq to be held in the middle of June.

> With the global COVID-19 pandemic raging and plummeting oil revenues, threatening an Iraqi economic collapse, it's important that our two governments work together to stop any reversal of the gains we've made in our efforts to defeat ISIS and stabilize the country.
>
> The Strategic Dialogue will be led by my Under Secretary for Political Affairs David Hale.
>
> And all strategic issues between our two countries will be on the agenda, including the future presence of the United States forces in that country, and how best to support an independent and sovereign Iraq.'[1]

Trump has said that there would be consequences if the U.S. forces in Iraq are removed, in the wake of Soleimani's killing. He argued that Iraq would have to repay money spent

1. ______(2020) 'Secretary Michael R. Pompeo Remarks To The Press, United States Department Of State', *state.gov.* [online]. Available at: https://www.state.gov/secretary-michael-r-pompeo-remarks-to-the-press-8/ [Accessed 21 June 2020].

on a major airbase in the west of Iraq, and he would impose stringent sanctions on them as he had done with Iran. By contrast, Iraqi Prime Minister Adel Abdul Mahdi said the killing of Soleimani was a breach of its national sovereignty. The Iraqi parliament had voted 170 to 0 to expel U.S. forces of nearly 5,000 from Iraq. However, it was a nonbinding vote, since under Iraqi constitutional law cabinet must formulate legislation (it cannot originate in parliament) (Pettyjohn, 2020b).

One associated question concerns the status and rights U.S. troops have in Iraq. After the 2003 occupation of Iraq, the Iraqi government invited U.S. troops to return to Iraq in 2014 to fight ISIS. However many Iraqis perceive U.S. troops as 'occupiers'. Responding to this public sentiment, PM Abdul Mahdi said that no U.S. bases would remain in Iraq (Pettyjohn, 2020a). With this in mind, some observers say the continuing U.S. military presence in Iraq is because Trump has no regional or country-specific strategy. Indeed, the stated official purposes seem incompatible with policies or justifications for U.S. military operations when the U.S. seems to be drifting into a violent confrontation with Iran on Iraqi soil, which could jeopardize the building of relations between Washington and Baghdad. Since 2003, some of Washington's Iraqi policies seem not to connect with strategic statements made. The U.S. government claims that its relationship, since the fall of Saddam Hussein, has focused on building and sustaining a stable and democratic country in Iraq.[1] However, at times there has been a deviation from this path, most egregiously when in 2010, the Obama administration attempted to cement Maliki's 'contested' election victory, which was secured through undemocratic means (Khederi, 2014).

In international security policy, the relationship between Washington and Baghdad centres on 'collective action problems'. So, Iraq and

1. ________(2020) 'Rebuilding Iraq: U.S. Achievements Through The Iraq Relief And Reconstruction Fund,' *United States of America State Department,2001-2009. state.gov.* [online] Available at: https://2001-2009.state.gov/p/nea/rls/rpt/60857.htm [Accessed 25 June 2020].

the U.S. share the responsibility and cooperate in managing the challenges of re-building the country. Also, regional partners, like Turkey and the Arab Gulf States, will be required to play a role. But even this approach, which has been a cornerstone of all the U.S. administrations in Iraq, is not without risk (Smith, 2017, p.55). For example, tensions between the Sunni and Shi'a political elites (Iran, Syrian leaders, Iraqi Shi'as, Yemeni Shi'as and Hizballah against numerous Sunni nations and groups) make the Middle East unstable and a security threat to U.S. interests. It is a dilemma for Trump and his neo-isolationist thinking, just as it presented a challenge to Obama with his cautious strategy to Iraq. Moreover, Trump would have to liaise with Russia (and China) on regional security in the Middle East (Vaisse and Porter, 2018, p.401). What is interesting in this case is that Obama, unlike Trump, was willing to open up a detente with Syria and Iran, albeit short-lived.

As of 2020, four possible scenarios exist for

the U.S. troop withdrawal:

- Limited withdrawal option: should ISIS be neutralised, the U.S. military can complete a gradual withdrawal. However, some forces can stay and shift from a combat to a training and advisory role.
- Extensive withdrawal option: almost all U.S. personnel, except a contingent to protect the U.S. embassy and a small group of advisors within Baghdad, largely to advise on military affairs.
- Full withdrawal option: all tactical ground and air forces and advisors are pulled out; all military 'shared bases' in Iraq given to the Iraqi government.
- Disengagement option: in addition to the above 'full withdrawal option', Trump ends all physical and financial military support to Iraq (Connable, 2020, p.6).

The above 'limited withdrawal option' and 'extensive withdrawal option' are less problematic for U.S. strategic interests. The 'disengagement option' and 'full withdrawal' option would be counterproductive to U.S. strategic interests, which shall be explored further below.

3.3 Trump and counter-terrorism in Iraq

Since 2003, the United States government has desired to quickly transform Iraq from an authoritarian regime to a functioning liberal-capitalist democracy (Keegan and Piggott, 2010). Nevertheless, recent history (indeed since the U.S. withdrawal of 2011) has shown that Washington's recent objectives are more associated with counter-terrorism and small unit deployments (special forces). Washington is not interested in propping up an ineffective Baghdad government or getting involved in nation-state building. The trend from nation-building to counter-terrorism materialised after the failure of the U.S.-led coalition to create lasting stability in a post-Saddam Iraq (Greenstock, 2016, p.423).

Trump in 2016 repeatedly blamed Obama for instability in the Middle East and the rise of ISIS in Iraq. During a speech in November 2015, President Trump asserted that the United States was failing in the war on terror. Trump rejected the idea of regime change and nation-building abroad. He called on U.S. allies to do more and proposed 'ideological warfare' against Muslim radicalism (Conley, 2018, p.66).

During the Washington summit, held in 2017 for countering terrorism, the secretary of state Mr Tillerson reported to the representatives of 68 allied countries that joint efforts were needed to defeat ISIS. The American administration clarified the stages of this defeat: firstly, primary military operations, the elimination of ISIS, and the restoration of the lands it controlled. Secondly, the restoration of stability, which includes re-building liberated cities and the return of essential services to the affected population. However, Trump says Iraq and local governments must re-build

Iraq with the support of Baghdad. They are responsible for removing war debris, removing landmines, and restoring water and electricity. Thirdly, the goal is to grow civil society and work to counter extremist ideology.

Trump seeks to keep within the realm of his neo-isolationist policy, involvement on the ground is kept to a minimum. In Trump's speech on 21 August 2017, he declared that American strategy to combat terrorism in Iraq would use military force to defeat it. However, keeping to his neo-realist and off-shore creed, he does not seek to '*construct democracies in faraway lands*' (Starr-Deelen, 2018, loc. 705-1295).

In the struggle against terrorists, Trump wants to avoid high-level and persistent military commitments. At the same time, he allows the Pentagon to use force and state finances against the jihadists. Trump's isolationist doctrine will see the U.S. military pull-back from its power projections abroad. It does not imply that Washington will cease playing a major international role as, after all, it is the dominant international power. Cooperative security implies that the United States will be the key actor working with international security institutions and allies against terrorists: mixing both U.S. realism and liberalism (Alejandro, 2006, p.137).

The now-deceased ISIS leader Abu Bakr al-Baghdadi declared a caliphate through very violent methods against the Iraqi people and its regional allies, and moderate Sunnis and Shiite Muslims. Trump argued that ISIS was a security threat to America's homeland and a threat to its Middle East interests. The elimination of ISIS became a primary goal of U.S. foreign policy (Mansbach, 2019, p.122). Indeed, Obama and Trump differ starkly from Bush's approach of armed regime change and his 'with us or against us' or 'coalition of the willing', neo-conservative influenced, administration post-9/11.

Although today ISIS no longer occupies the vast areas of northern and western Iraq, it is still a security threat to Washington and Baghdad's interests (Blanchard and Humud, 2018, p.4). In the face of external and internal threats, Iraq struggles to protect itself and is still dependent upon U.S. security forces, as well as other local allies (Sky, 2015, p.267). Of the latter, there is a consensus that local allies are not prepared to continue the mission without Washington carrying most of the financial and military burden.

At the same time, counter-terrorism is a priority concern for Trump's administration (Lesser, 2020). The U.S. administration has effectively defeated ISIS, but still faces some threat from global Salafi jihadism (Krieg, 2017, pp.139-158). Despite this, Trump's doctrine of realism and neo-isolationism sees a minimal role for the U.S. forces across the world. He looks to allies to assist strategically in the 'war on terrorism' (Douthat, 2020).

Trump and Obama share two similarities here, firstly a desire to build broader international coalitions against terror—and in the belief that the United States and its values and civilisation form a moral and military campaign against global terrorists.

President Barack Obama

In office

January 20, 2009 – January 20, 2017

Conclusion

This book has analysed the foreign policy of the Obama and Trump administrations on Iraq. It considered whether the policies of each leader had a negative or positive impact or both on Iraqi national security. The primary research question asked: *What drives the United States' relationship with Iraq*? Secondary research questions addressed: *What are the national interests and ideology involved? How do Obama and Trump's views of national in-*

terest differ, and why? How does this influence troop pull-out and counter-terrorism in Iraq? In conclusion, it is apparent that the hegemonic protector of the 'free world', the United States, both assisted and hindered the national security of Iraq. In the wake of Bush's devastating 2003 war in Iraq, the U.S.-led reconstruction of the society was flawed and lacked commitment. Unlike the Western European allies after the Second World War, there was no Marshall Plan for Iraq with a committed Washington elite behind it. However, on balance, Washington's role in defeating ISIS has been positive for Iraqis.

President Obama

⊙ Foreign policy: Middle East

The weaknesses of President Obama's foreign policy were influenced by Bush's unpopular war. During Obama's leadership, the Middle East policy was based on a 'lead from behind' approach and the containment of immediate threats. He requested allies to help resolve conflicts and promoted burden-sharing proposals. On the other hand, he was against U.S. military intervention in further conflicts like Syria, and as noted, reluctant to get the U.S. military back into conflict-ridden Iraq. This is remarkably similar to the position of Donald Trump, despite strongly differing ideological justifications given by both presidents.

Driven by his liberal-democratic mindset, Obama wished to withdraw from Iraq, and encourage it to be a sovereign, democratising country with a sustainable liberal economy. However, the reconstruction plan for Iraq, after 2003, was not implemented effectively and efficiently. The post-war reconstruction failings were acknowledged by the Special Inspector General for Iraq Reconstruction, 2011.[1]

The 2011 U.S. military withdrawal saw politics in Iraq move away from accountable and representative government towards competing power groups and identity politics. This was shown by the occurrence of inter-communal conflicts and suspicion between different sects

1. ___________(2013) 'Special Inspector General for Iraq Reconstruction: Final Report to U.S. Congress', *DTIC*, 9 September. Available at: https://apps.dtic.mil/dtic/tr/fulltext/u2/a592228.pdf (15 August 2020).

of Islam and ethnic groups.

Obama's troop pull-out

The departure of the U.S. military created a power vacuum in Iraq; it allowed for ISIS to spill over from the civil war in Syria and to control regions in Iraq. The pull-out in 2011 also saw the reduction of U.S financial support, training, equipment, and intelligence information. There is a strong correlation between the withdrawal of the U.S. military personnel and the inability of the Iraqis to handle the political and economic crises. The societal and ethnic problems led to the collapse of the Iraqi army and police forces. As a result, the cities of Mosul and Anbar, and some other Iraqi provinces, were occupied by ISIS (until its defeat in 2017).

Obama on counter-terrorism

Obama's Iraq policy focused on combating terrorism (and on preventing terrorists from attacking the U.S. homeland). To combat 'terrorists' he used large numbers of drone strikes. These were supported by intelligence operations and security cooperation. This approach avoided direct military intervention. He was conscious not to repeat the heavy-handed and unpopular methods of warfare deployed by Bush. However, the drone strikes raise ethical questions of proportionality, justification and reasonableness; for example, do they conform with liberal values about human life? If a target is wrongly selected, inevitably unarmed civilians, and perhaps children will be the victims (and sometimes entire wedding parties). Obama's counter-terrorism strategy and use of drones have left worry in the minds of liberal-Westerners and many Iraqis. It would be incorrect to say Obama would not use violence when it serviced the pressing interests and power of the United States.

While Obama adopted a less macho and more cautious strategy to Iraq than Bush and Trump, the long-term power interests and objectives of the United States in Iraq persisted much the same. Although Obama fulfilled his pledge to withdraw U.S. troops, the promises regarding Iraq's economic development, security and national unity remain problematic. In review, expectations were too high, going far beyond what could have been reasonably achieved. Obama's involvement in Iraq was limited because of domestic issues in the United States. So, we can say U.S. economic and social crises were affecting national politics and foreign policy.

Furthermore, new challenges were prioritised over Iraq and ISIS, like the growing power of the Chinese Communist Party and its turn to technological-authoritarianism and nationalism. The 'revolutions' in Egypt, Libya, and Tunisia caught Washington by surprise. Equally, the actions of Russia's Putin, including espionage, and his bombing campaign in Syria, concerned Obama.

President Donald Trump

In office
January 20, 2017 – January 20, 2021

President Trump

⊙ Criticism of neo-realism

The realist theory explains international relations from one side, which is about war and conflict and balance of power. It does not fully explore other aspects of I.R., like cooperation maintained by international soft power relations and trade. Also, factors like the presence of international institutions that enhance trust, and help resolve political problems (like those in Northern Ireland), and spread of democracy and human rights. These liberal concepts have a role in enhancing security too. Focusing on domestic interests only and an isolationist policy of retrenchment, the United States will, surely, increase the complexity of the challenges, especially in the Middle East in general and Iraq in particular.

In this respect, Trump's criticism of U.S. involvement in the Middle East, sometimes backed-up by prejudice views about Arabs and Muslims, is risky for the country's national interests. This is in contrast to Obama's more even-handed policy of fostering stable relations with countries like Iraq while keeping military involvement to a minimum.

Foreign policy: Middle East

Trump's foreign policy towards the Middle East is based on the doctrine of 'business deals'. He has followed the mechanisms of supply and demand in dealing with countries in the region in a way that strengthens Washington's position without paying any price to protect its partners (the sale of armaments to Saudi Arabia). Instead, they are the ones who must pay in exchange for U.S. protection. On this basis, Trump is less interested in democratisation and human rights in the Middle East, pursuing a mercantilist strategy instead.

Trump has reduced the level of U.S. intervention in the Middle East and is refocusing national attention on threats from Russia and Iran. However, his main target is the Chinese Communist Party. In particular, since COVID-19, China is the number one target of Trump's containment policy. In fact, it was Obama started this foreign policy reassessment, and he termed it: 'pivot to the East (China)'.

Trump's Iraq policy and troop pull-out

So, Iraq is not a priority for the Trump administration. Simultaneously, with the United States increasingly seeking to influence medium-level regional actors, the U.S. administration uses Iraq to resolve other regional issues in terms of balancing power with Russia and limiting Iranian influence, albeit at the expense of Iraqi interests.

Trump's policy, like that of the Obama administration, seems torn between wanting to appear and act tough on terrorism and America's adversaries, while at the same time wanting to pull back from Iraq (and military commitments in Europe). In early 2019, for example, Trump remarked that some U.S. forces should remain in Iraq to 'watch Iran', but that the United States should withdraw most forces because they could return if necessary. This latter view is remarkably similar to the views of Obama, in that both presidents viewed the United States withdrawal from Iraq unproblematic for Iraq's security and reconstruction, despite evidence that Iraqi forces were relying on U.S. intelligence support, training, and logistics.

Furthermore, Trump's policy needs to be revised in terms of continued U.S. military and economic support to Iraq. Furthermore, there has been recent tension in the relationship between Baghdad and Washington. The Iraqi parliament decided to expel American forces, as a result of the 2020 assassination of the deputy commander of the Iraqi Popular Mobilization Forces, Abo Mahdi Al-Muhandis and the Iranian General Kasim Soleimani. But this comes with issues. The withdrawal of the U.S. forces from Iraq might increase the rise of jihadists—and undermine the international effort to combat terrorism. It might increase Iranian influence, a state which Trump considers to be one of Washington's adversaries. It might increase the role of Putin and Russia. Furthermore, it would allow China to gain more economic control. Indeed, this would work against the United States interests in the Middle East.

Trump on counter-terrorism

Arguably, isolationism is not Trump's only stance, because he used hard power against

ISIS. Trump's attitude against ISIS was aggressive, and he was willing to destroy the organisation quickly. This was undertaken despite his administration's move away from commitments in the Middle East.

Trump has a nationalist and populist approach to U.S. politics, unlike the liberal-global outlook of Obama. Trump praises the nation-state and considers it central in his policy, and national interests above all else. Trump's handling of foreign policy is linked to how Washington is involved in world events and conflicts in general, and the Middle East region in particular—and the value of economic interests that can be achieved from that linkage. It was shown in his statements regarding the necessity of reviewing cooperation with NATO, and in the defence contributions of friendly countries. Also, he is critical of unbridled globalisation. Yet, he is unable to admit that political and strategic interests are based on the principle of mutual interests and trust, and not solely on a country's self-interest.

Trump does not favour the idea of humanitarian intervention as a basis for interference in the internal affairs of other states. Trump believes that there is no need for U.S. forces or foreign policy to be involved in others affairs (off-shore balancing) unless there is a threat to U.S. interests and national security. That is confirmed by Trump's statements about the Middle East. Trump's realist approach places interest over classical liberal values. He tends towards stability between states. Also, he has a negative attitude towards some Muslim societies. It is in contrast, with the 'building bridges' approach that characterised Obama, and his promotion of democracy, the support of freedom, the spreading of human rights. It was seen during the events of the so-called Arab Spring, and in the hand of friendship, Obama offered to both democratic and authoritarian Muslim-majority states (like Iran).

Trump's administration is monitoring the growing Chinese Communist Party, and Russia, and the Iranian role in the Middle East region. However, in the Middle East he seeks to create a state of balance in terms of cost and what may be achieved from direct intervention options. For Trump, foreign policy should be in support of the interests of the United States, and it is evident in the rhetoric that Trump uses in his speeches to win over U.S. voters.

The retreat of the United States from assisting the reconstruction of Iraq might lead to the re-growth and re-emergence of terrorist groups (as well as undermine other international efforts to combat terrorism). A stable, prosperous and democratic Iraq is important for the peace in the region. Also, there is a moral argument that Washington should assist Iraq because of the impact of Bush's war on Iraqi civilians. However, Iraq needs to be distanced from being involved in any U.S. conflicts with other regional actors, like Iran.

Iraqi leaders need to reach out to their diverse and young population, encourage them to participate in official decision-making, and integrate ethnic and sectarian plurality around a universal national identity. Resources need to be distributed equally and fairly. In doing so, the Iraqi government will move closer to cementing its legitimacy in the hearts and minds of the citizenry that it serves. Likewise, Iraq will attain greater sovereign control, and would become a reliable partner to sceptical U.S. presidents. Finally, events in Iraq will continue to impact upon U.S. national interests, so, Washington will probably remain involved in the country for some time to come.

To be continued ......

President Joe Biden and Vice President Kamala Harris

President Joe Biden

In office since

January 20,2021

Bibliography

Primary sources: U.S. Government online

1. _______(2013) 'President Obama in Address to the United Nations General Assembly', *White House Website*. 23 September. Available at: https://obamawhitehouse.archives.gov/the-press-office/2013/09/24/remarks-president-obama-address-united-nations-general-assembly (Accessed 15 August 2020).

2. ___________(2013) 'Special Inspector General for Iraq Reconstruction: Final Re-

port to U.S. Congress', *DTIC*, 9 September. Available at: https://apps.dtic.mil/dtic/tr/fulltext/u2/a592228.pdf (15 August 2020).

3. ________(2014) 'President Obama Makes a Statement on the Crisis in Iraq', *Obama White House Archives.gov.* 14 August. Available at: https://obamawhitehouse.archives.gov/blog/2014/08/07/president-obama-makes-statement-iraq (Accessed 15 August 2020).

4. _________(2014) 'White House Office of the Press Secretary. Statement by the U.S. President on Iraq', *Obama Whitehouse. Archives. gov.* 13 June. Available at: https://obamawhitehouse.archives.gov/the-press-office/2014/06/13/statement-president-iraq (accessed 15 August 2020).

5. ______(2020) 'Secretary Michael R. Pompeo Remarks To The Press - United States of America Department Of State', *state.gov.* [online] Available at: https://www.state.gov/secretary-michael-r-pompeo-remarks-to-the-press-8/ [Accessed 21 June 2020].

6. ________(2015) 'Remarks By The President In State Of The Union Address', *Whitehouse.gov*, January 20. [online] Available

at: https://obamawhitehouse.archives.gov/the-press-office/2015/01/20/remarks-president-state-union-address-January-20-2015 [Accessed 4 July 2020].

7. __________(2020) 'Rebuilding Iraq: U.S. Achievements Through The Iraq Relief And Reconstruction Fund,' *United States of America State Department, 2001-2009. state.gov.* [online]. Available at: https://2001-2009.state.gov/p/nea/rls/rpt/60857.htm [Accessed 25 June 2020].

8. FY 1999-2000, 'Department of State Performance Plan National Interests', *U.S. Government* [online] Available at: https://1997-2001.state.gov/global/general_foreign_policy/00_perf_1.pdf (Accessed 10 June 2020).

9. Allison, G. (2020) 'America's National Interests' *NCJRS Abstract – The Commission of America's National Interest. National Criminal Justice Reference Service. NCJRS.gov. The United States.* [online] Available at: https://www.ncjrs.gov/App/publications/Abstract.aspx?id=189698 (Accessed 10 June 2020).

10. Blanchard, C. and Humud, C. (2018) 'The Islamic State and U.S. Policy'. *Congres-*

sional Research Service [online] Fas.org. Available at: https://fas.org/sgp/crs/mideast/R43612.pdf [Accessed 27 June 2020], p. 4.

11. Brzezinski, Z. (1997) *The Grand Chessboard*. USA: Basic Books, pp.23-24. [online]. Available at: https://www.cia.gov/library/abbottabad-compound/36/36669B7894E857AC4F3445EA646BFFE1_Zbigniew_Brzezinski_-_The_Grand_ChessBoard.doc.pdf (Accessed 12 June 2020).
12. *Congressional Record* (2014) *United States of America Senate*. Vol. 160, pt 8, June 23, pp.11127. [online] Available at: https://books.google.co.uk/books?id=1V5cpDql_eUC&printsec=frontcover&source=gbs_ge_summary_r&cad=0#v=onepage&q&f=false (Accessed 16 June 2020).
13. Gunaratna R, *Terrorist Trends and Analyses*, (December 2015 - January 2016), Vol. 8, No. 1 pp. 6-11. [online] Available at: https://css.ethz.ch/content/dam/ethz/special-interest/gess/cis/center-for-securities-studies/resources/docs/RSIS%20CTTA-January-2016.pdf [Accessed 19 June 2020].
14. International Institute for Strategic Studies

(IISS) (2020) *Military Balance 2020*. London: Routledge, p.45.

15. 'National Security Strategy of the United States of America'. (2017) *The White House. gov*. Available at: https://www.whitehouse.gov/wp-content/uploads/2017/12/NSS-Final-12-18-2017-0905.pdf (Accessed 15 August 2020).

16. Manyin, Mark E.; Daggett, Stephen; Dolven, Ben; Lawrence, Susan V.; Martin, Michael F.; O'Rourke, Ronald et al. (2012) 'Pivot to the Pacific? The Obama Administration's 'Rebalancing' Toward Asia', report, 28 March; Washington D.C. (https://digital.library.unt.edu/ark:/67531/metadc86617/, University of North Texas Libraries, UNT Digital Library, https://digital.library.unt.edu; crediting UNT Libraries Government Documents Department, p.4. (Accessed 18 June 2020).

17. *National Security Strategies of the United States of America*. (2015) Obama Whitehouse Archives, p.180. [online] Available at: https://obamawhitehouse.archives.gov/sites/default/files/docs/2015_national_security_strategy_2.pdf (Accessed 16 June 2020).

18. *National Strategy For Counterterrorism Of The United States Of America*. (2018) Whitehouse, Washington, pp.1-35. [online] Available at: https://www.google.com/search?q=national+strategy+for+counterterrorism+of+the+united+states+of+america+october+2018&rlz=1C1GGRV_enGB750GB750&oq=National+Strategy+for+Counterterrorism+of+the+United+States+of+America+october&aqs=chrome.0.0j69i57.9945j0j7&sourceid=chrome&ie=UTF-8 [Accessed 19 June 2020].

19. Obama, Barack (2010) 'Address before a Joint Session of the Congress on the State of the Union', January 27, cited in *Obama Whitehouse Archives.gov*. [online] Available at: https://obamawhitehouse.archives.gov/the-press-office/remarks-president-state-union-address (Accessed 16 June 2020).

20. Obama, Barack. (2011) 'Remarks by the President on Afghanistan', June 22, cited in *Obama Whitehouse Archives.gov*. 2020. [online] Available at: https://obamawhitehouse.archives.gov/the-press-office/2011/06/22/remarks-president-way-forward-Afghanistan (Accessed 13 June 2020).

21. Obama, Barack. (2015) 'U.S.- Gulf Cooperation Council Camp David Joint Statement', 14 May 2015, cited in *Obama Whitehouse Archives.gov. The White House United States*. [online] Available at: https://obamawhitehouse.archives.gov/reality-check/the-press-office/2015/05/14/us-gulf-cooperation-council-camp-david-joint-statement [Accessed 15 June 2020].

22. U.S. Department of State, 2009-2017, *Patterns of Global Terrorism*. President Bush address to Congress on September 20, 2001, Washington. [online] Available at: https://2009-2017.state.gov/j/ct/rls/pgtrpt/index.htm [Accessed 19 June 2020].

Lectures and talks

23. Singh Robert. 'The US and the Middle East.' Lecture: Birkbeck Uni, London, 3 April 2019.

Secondary sources: books, journal articles and online

24. ________ (2020) The International Institute for Strategic Studies (IISS) *Military Balance 2020*. London: Routledge.

25. ________Ref no. 48: 'Lexington', *Economist*, December 1 (2012), cited in Dueck, C. (2015) *The Obama Doctrine: Grand Strategy Today*. New York: Oxford University Press.

26. Alejandro, C. (2006) *The War on Terrorism and the American "Empire" after the Cold War*. London: Taylor and Francis. Kindle Edition.

27. Baylis, J., Smith, S. and Owens, P. (2017) *The Globalization Of World Politics*. 7th ed. New York: Oxford University Press.

28. Brands, H. (2018) *American Grand Strategy in the Age of Trump*, Washington: Brookings Institution Press.

29. Brennan, P. (2014) 'No, U.S. Troops Did Not Have to Leave Iraq', *National Review*, 16 June. [online] Available at: https://www.nationalreview.com/corner/no-us-troops-didnt-have-leave-iraq-patrick-brennan/ (Accessed 18 June 2020).

30. Brown, G.T. & McLean, I, & McMillan, A. (eds.) (2018) *Oxford Concise Dictionary of Politics and International Relations*. London: Oxford University Press, pp. 324-25.

31. Conley, R., 2018. *Presidential Leadership*

and National Security. New York: Routledge.

32. Connable, Ben, James Dobbins, Howard J. Shatz, Raphael S. Cohen, and Becca Wasser. (2020) 'Weighing U.S. Troop Withdrawal from Iraq: Strategic Risks and Recommendations', *Rand Corporation*, Santa Monica, California: Rand. [online] Available at: https://www.rand.org/pubs/perspectives/PE362.html [Accessed 23 June 2020].
33. Copeland, D. (1997) 'Foreign policy, Foreign Service and the 21st. Century: The challenge of globalization', *Canadian Foreign Policy Journal*, 4(3), pp.105-112.
34. Cordesman, A. (2020). 'Ending America's Grand Strategic Failures', *Center for Strategic and International Studies.org*. [online] Available at: https://www.csis.org/analysis/ending-americas-grand-strategic-failures [Accessed 24 June 2020].
35. Cox, M. & Stokes, D. (eds.) (2012) *US Foreign Policy*. London: Oxford University Press.
36. Cronin, A. (2012) 'U.S. Grand Strategy and Counterterrorism.' *Orbis*, 56(2), pp.192-214.

37. Deudney, Daniel, Ikenberry, John. (2017) 'Realism, Liberalism and the Iraq War.' 16 January 2017. Survival. Volume 59, Issue 4. Page no? Available at: https://www.tandfonline.com/doi/full/10.1080/00396338.2017.1349757 (Accessed?)

38. Dixit, A. and Nalebuff, B. (1993) *Thinking Strategically*. New York: W.W. Norton.

39. Dodge, T. (2012) *Iraq: From War to a New Authoritarianism*. London: The International Institute for Strategic Studies, Loc 2228 of 4121 Kindle Edition.

40. Douthat, R. (2020) *Opinion: The Trump Doctrine*. *Nytimes.com*. [online] Available at: https://www.nytimes.com/2019/01/29/opinion/trump-doctrine-venezuela-afghanistan.html?action=click&module=Opinion&pgtype=Homepage [Accessed 27 June 2020].

41. Dueck, C. (2015) *The Obama Doctrine: Grand Strategy Today*. New York: Oxford University Press.

42. Dunne,T., Kurki, M. and Smith, S. (2016) *International Relations Theories, Discipline and Diversity,* Oxford University Press.

43. Fawaz A. Gerges. (2013) 'The Obama ap-

proach to the Middle East: the end of America's moment?', *International Affairs*, 89: 2, (March).

44. Gelb, L.H. (2012) 'The Elusive Obama Doctrine', *The National Interest*, no. 121 (September/October), pp. 18-28, p. 20. [online] Available at: www.jstor.org/stable/42896546 (Accessed 13 June 2020).

45. Glaser, John, and Trevor Thrall. (2017) 'Obama's Foreign Policy Legacy and the Myth of Retrenchment'. *Cato Institute*, 24 April, www.jstor.org/stable/resrep04989 (Accessed 16 June 2020).

46. Greenstock, S. (2016) *Iraq: The Cost of War*. London: William Heinemann Ltd.

47. Hannah, J., and Zarif, M. (2020) 'The U.S.-Iraqi Relationship Is Coming to a Head—and That's a Good Thing', *Foreign policy.com*, May 2020. https://foreignpolicy.com/2020/05/04/united-states-iraq-iran-relationship/ (5 July 2020).

48. Hunt, M. (1988) *Ideology and U.S. Foreign Policy*. New Haven: Yale University Press.

49. Hunt, M. H. (2009) *The American Ascendancy*. North Carolina: Univ of North Carolina Press.

50. Khederi, Ali. 2014. 'Why we stuck with Maliki- and lost Iraq.' *The Washington Post*. 13 July. https://www.washingtonpost.com/opinions/why-we-stuck-with-maliki--and-lost-iraq/2014/07/03/0dd6a8a4-f7ec-11e3-a606-946fd632f9f1_story.html (Accessed 15 August 2020).

51. Indyk, M. S., Lieberthal, K. G. and O'Hanlon, M. E. (2012) 'Scoring Obama's Foreign Policy: A Progressive Pragmatist Tries to Bend History', *Foreign Affairs*, 91(3), pp. 29–43. Available at: http://search.ebscohost.com/login.aspx?direct=true&site=eds-live&scope=site&db=edshol&AN=edshol.hein.journals.fora91.49 (Accessed: 13 June 2020).

52. Jenkins, B.M. (2017) 'Bush, Obama, And Trump: The Evolution of U.S. Counterterrorist Policy Since 9/11', *International Institute for Counter-Terrorism*, pp. 1-5. [online] Available at: https://www.rand.org/pubs/external_publications/EP67340.html [Accessed 19 June 2020].

53. Jones, S and Libicki, M. (2007) *How Terrorist Groups End. Lessons for Countering al Qa'ida*. USA: Rand Corporation.

54. Kahl. H.C. (2014) 'No, Obama Did not

Lose Iraq', *Politico Magazine*, 15 June. [online] Available at: https://www.politico.com/magazine/story/2014/06/no-obama-didnt-lose-iraq-107874 (Accessed 18 June 2020).

55. Kayser, Courtney (2015) 'The Power of Ideas in Politics: Social Constructivism and Obama's Foreign Policy in Iraq', *Political Analysis*, Vol. 17, pp. 6-12.

56. Keegan, J. and Piggott, R. (2010) *The Iraq War*. London: Hutchinson. Kindle Edition.

57. King, E. (2016) *Obama, The Media, and Framing the U.S. Exit From Iraq and Afghanistan*. London: Routledge.

58. Krieg, A. (2017) 'Trump and the Middle East: "Barking Dogs Seldom Bite".' *Insight Turkey*, 19(3), pp.139-158.

59. Lawson, G., and Robbie Shilliam. (2010) 'Sociology and International Relations: Legacies and Prospects,' *Cambridge Review of International Affairs*. 23(1) pp. 69-86; 75, 82.

60. Lesser, I. (2020) 'What to Expect from the United States: A Look Ahead at US Foreign Policy', *Istituto Affari Internazionali (IAI)* [online] Available at: http://193.61.13.36

on Sat, 27 Jun 2020 [Accessed 27 June 2020].

61. Lindsay, James M. (2011) 'George W. Bush, Barack Obama and the Future of US Global Leadership', *International Affairs (Royal Institute of International Affairs 1944-)*, (87/4), pp. 765–779. *JSTOR*, www.jstor.org/stable/20869758 (Accessed 18 June 2020).

62. MacDonald, P. (2018) *Twilight of The Titans*. New York: Cornell University Press.

63. MacDonald, P. (2018a) 'America First? Explaining Continuity and Change in Trump's Foreign Policy', *Political Science Quarterly*, 133(3).

64. Magcamit, M. (2017) 'Explaining the Three-Way Linkage Between Populism, Securitization, And Realist Foreign Policies: President Donald Trump and the Pursuit of "America First" Doctrine', *World Affairs*, 180(3), pp.6-35.

65. Mansbach, R. and McCormick, J. (2019) *Foreign Policy Issues For America*. New York: Routledge.

66. Mann, J. (2012) *The Obamians*. New York: Viking.

67. Marshall, T. (2019) *Prisoners of Geography*. London: Elliott and Thompson.

68. Mason, Jeff. (2014) 'Obama does not rule out airstrikes against Iraq insurgents', *Reuters*, 12 June. Available at: https://in.reuters.com/article/us-iraq-security-obama/obama-does-not-rule-out-air-strikes-against-iraq-insurgents-idUKKBN0EN1V720140612 (Accessed 15 August 2020).

69. McCrisken, Trevor. (2011) 'Ten years on: Obama's war on terrorism in rhetoric and practice', *International Affairs*, 87, no. 4 (July): 781- 801.

70. Mead, W. (2009) 'America's Sticky Power', *Foreign Policy*. [online] Available at: https://foreignpolicy.com/2009/10/29/americas-sticky-power/ [Accessed 4 July 2020].

71. Mejia, Zameena. (2017) 'Barack Obama left Donald Trump a letter before leaving office. Here's what he said', 3 Sept. *CNBC.COM*. [online]. Available at:

72. https://www.cnbc.com/2017/09/03/obama-sent-trump-a-letter-before-leaving-office-heres-what-he-said.html (Accessed 18 June 2020).

73. Nuechterlein, D. (1976) 'National interests and foreign policy: A conceptual framework for analysis and decision-making', *British Journal of International Studies*, 2(3), pp.246-266.

74. Pettyjohn, S. (2020a) 'Can Iraq Evict U.S. Forces?' *Rand.org*. [online] Available at: https://www.rand.org/blog/2020/01/can-iraq-evict-us-forces.html [Accessed 25 June 2020].

75. Pettyjohn, S. (2020b) 'Trump Threatens "Sanctions Like They've Never Seen" If Iraq Evicts U.S. Forces. Can Iraq Do It? It's Likely That Iraq Will Expel U.S. Forces.' *Washington Post.com* [online] Available at: https://www.washingtonpost.com/politics/2020/01/06/trump-threatens-sanctions-like-theyve-never-seen-if-iraq-evicts-us-forces-can-iraq-do-it/ [Accessed 21 June 2020].

76. Pilecki, A., Muro, J. M., Hammack, P. L., & Clemons, C. M. (2014). 'Moral exclusion and the justification of U.S. counter-terrorism strategy: Bush, Obama, and the terrorist enemy figure', *Peace and Conflict: Journal of Peace Psychology, 20*(3), 285–299. [online] Available: https://doi.org/10.1037/

pac0000030 (Accessed 20 June 2020).

77. Rogin, Josh. (2011), *Foreign Polcy. com*. Available at: https://foreignpolicy.com/2011/10/21/how-the-obama-administration-bungled-the-iraq-withdrawal-negotiations/ (Accessed 15 August 2020).

78. Santos, M. and Teixeira, U. (2015) 'Interests and Values in Obama's Foreign Policy: Leading from Behind?'. *Revista Brasileira de Política Internacional*, 58(2), pp.119-145. [online] Available at: https://www.scielo.br/scielo.php?script=sci_arttext&pid=S0034-73292015000200119 (Accessed 18 June 2020).

79. Schweller, R. (2018) 'Three Cheers for Trump's Foreign Policy: What the Establishment Misses', *Foreign Affairs*, 97, September/October. [online] Available: https://www.foreignaffairs.com/articles/world/2018-08-14/three-cheers-trumps-foreign-policy (Accessed 20 June 2020).

80. Singh, R. (2016) *After Obama: Renewing American Leadership, Restoring Global Order*, New York: Cambridge University Press.

81. Sink, J. and Carey, G. (2020) 'Trump Says Now 'Isn't The Right Point' For U.S.

Troops To Pull Out Of Iraq', *Time.com* [online] Time. Available at: https://time.com/5760864/trump-us-troops-iraq/ [Accessed 25 June 2020].

82. Smith, M. (2017) *International Security*. 2nd ed. London: Palgrave.

83. Sky, Emma. (2015) *The Unravelling: High Hopes and Missed Opportunities in Iraq*. USA: Atlantic Books. Kindle Edition.

84. Starr-Deelen, Donna, G. (2018) *Counter-Terrorism from the Obama Administration to President Trump*. London: Springer International Publishing. Kindle Edition. Loc 705- 1295.

85. Stern, J. (2015) 'Obama and Terrorism: Like It or Not, the War Goes On', *Foreign Affairs*, 94, (5) pp. 62-70. *JSTOR*. [online] Available at: www.jstor.org/stable/24483739 (Accessed 19 June 2020).

86. Terry, J. (2013) 'Change or more of the same? Obama and Iraq,' *International Journal of Contemporary Iraqi Studies*, 7(1), pp.43-54.

87. Tollast, Robert. (2016) 'The civil wars of Iraq's Sunni tribes.' *1001 Iraqi Thoughts*.com, 28 March. Available at:

https://1001iraqithoughts.com/2016/03/28/the-civil-wars-of-iraqs-sunni-tribes-fault-lines-within-8-sunni-tribes-and-sub-tribes-2003-2016/ (Accessed 15 August 2020).

88. Vaïsse, J. and Porter, C. (2018) *Zbigniew Brzezinski*. London: Harvard University Press.

89. Wendt, Alexander. (1995) 'Constructing International Politics,' *International Security* 20, no. 1 (Summer), pp. 71-81.

90. Wu, C. (2017) 'Understanding the Structures and Contents of National Interests: An Analysis of Structural Equation Modeling', *The Korean Journal of International Studies*, 15(3), pp.391-419.

91. Zarakol, Ayse. (2011) 'What Makes Terrorism Modern? Terrorism, Legitimacy, and the International System', *Review of International Studies*, 37(5), pp. 2311-2336.